6 FIGURE FREIGHT BROKER

How To Make $100,000+ As A Freight Broker In The Digital Age

TABLE OF CONTENTS

Introduction

I was sitting in the basement of my home playing Madden '11, and my younger brother mentioned that he was going to leave his current job to go to truck driving school. A place that I was three months behind on mortgage payments. I had exhausted loans from family members to make those mortgage payments. To put gas in the car for the week, my wife would negatively affect her bank account. We used her bank account because I couldn't get a bank account, and I was living payday loan to payday loan, which is worse than check to check. I was struggling as a real estate broker. I had only earned $12,000 in commissions that year, which sounds terrible until I add the fact that I had $15,000 in business expenses. I was on the brink of bankruptcy. I wasn't happy or in love with my wife, and I was on the edge of divorce. I was in a dark place after the passing of my mom. I had blown through an inheritance that included two free and clear homes, $35,000 in bank savings, and $150,000 in retirement savings. I was delusional about what I could accomplish with my 2011 mindset. I was horrible at making money, and worse yet, I was awful at saving money. So on the rare occasion where I did get my hands on some cash. I'd blow it. I had big dreams and big aspirations, but I didn't have a realistic plan to accomplish those goals. I was a bad fit for my chosen profession.

When I look at the world, I see dollar signs and opportunity. I knew that trucking would let me provide for my family—a primary goal of mine. But more importantly, trucking could give me a blueprint to build a million-dollar business.

Fast forward to Christmas Eve, and my wife told me she was having an affair with someone that was "not enough of a stranger" "and I moved in with my Aunt. So now I have no wife, no home. My only possession of any value was my car, a '91 Lexus LS 400. I loved that car, but like everything else in my life at the time. Everything was either broken or on its way to being broken. The car's engine overheated, and now I didn't even have a car. I forgot to mention that my license was about to be suspended in the next few weeks.

I fast forward to 15 months after several conversations about trucking with everyone I knew; I enrolled in truck driving school. I started down a path that would change my life. I went from not having enough to pay my bills to make so much money that I had to find smarter ways to spend my money. I remember two distinct phrases from that time. I spoke with an older gentleman at a bar who had his CDL, and he called it the "Blue Collar Degree," and my girlfriend at the time calling it my stupid truck obsession. Looking back on it, I was obsessed, and whenever you truly want to make life-altering changes, you have to be obsessed! As I continued my deep dive into trucking, I started to uncover the countless number of ways that someone could make money in trucking. The broader trucking industry falls under the logistics category. My earlier "6 Figure Trucking" focused on being a truck driver and owning a trucking company. This book will focus on the freight brokerage business within the logistics industry. Freight brokerages have just as many, if not more, opportunities in the industry. If you're looking to get into trucking but can't or don't want to be behind the wheel, then the freight brokerage business is a perfect option. Freight brokerage allows someone to earn a living in the industry without ever leaving their homes.

Now we'll look at the basics of the freight brokerage industry!

What do freight brokers do?

If you're new to the logistics industry and excited to study the business, or you're a truck driver that hates the long hauls that take you far away from your friends, then becoming a freight broker is a great option. As a freight broker, you create your hours, and depending on your dedication to the craft, you could make well over six figures.

Freight brokers are intermediaries that connect shippers with motor carriers who haul freight. Just like real estate brokers don't own the homes they sell, freight brokers don't own the freight they broker. They have the task of finding the most profitable and safest manner to get loads from origin to final destination.

Freight brokers are en vogue because businesses are more inclined to use intermediaries to assist them in hauling their freight. Carriers benefit because they have a reliable source to find freight to haul.

Currently, more than 16,000 freight brokers are working inside the United States.

While starting a successful freight brokerage may be achieved from the comfort of your home, there are necessary steps you must take to create a legal and profitable business.

Companies manufacture cargo that's delivered to various destinations. They pay a freight broker to move the freight; the broker will then pay a carrier to deliver the product. The broker retains a profit for providing this service; they are the vital link between shippers and carriers. You're thinking – "Why can't shippers connect with carriers directly and vice versa?" Although some carriers and shippers work directly with each other. Thus, cutting out the "middleman" For the most part, they both like to focus on what they do best. Shippers are more profitable when they focus on manufacturing their products, and carriers are more profitable when focusing on transporting freight. Some carriers broker and haul freight simultaneously, but they usually concentrate on perfecting one aspect of the business before diving into another.

As I stated earlier, a freight broker acts as a transportation middleman. They are neither a shipper nor a carrier; however, they play a vital role in the logistics industry. They're responsible for maintaining the communication line with the carrier to keep the shipper updated on information about their freight up to and including the final destination.

Brokers can run their very own business or work for a freight brokerage company. More often than not, freight brokerages only hire people who have an established "book of business"; or individuals that already have existing customers. Yup, you guessed it, you have to get experience to get the job, but you first need a job to gain experience. This is why many brokers start their own companies.

Freight brokers make it easier for shippers to discover reliable carriers to haul a load. The broker is responsible for every aspect of the shipment once they accept the contract. They must ensure the freight is picked up and delivered on time and stay in the same condition as it was at the beginning of the process.

Brokers offer a valuable service to motor companies and shippers. They help carriers fill their trucks and help shippers find reliable motor companies.

Additionally, it's common for a successful freight broker to grow their business; by creating revenue streams that provide different freight services. As stated earlier, the logistics industry's infinite number of possibilities makes it so appealing to a vast array of people. The logistics industry is vital in our country; it was declared an essential business during the Covid-19 pandemic that started at the end of 2019.

Some brokers prefer to use different companies to handle a wide range of operations. An example of this would be a factoring company that manages the expedited payment to carriers for services rendered.

Chapter 1: Freight Broker Salary Range & Skillset

Freight broker's income varies greatly.

These are the averages according to the following sources:

Indeed.com -- $51,032

LinkedIn -- $30,000-$83,000

Careeronestop.org -- $25,000-$65,000

Payscale.com -- $41,940-$143,000

These ranges depend on numerous factors, including experience, ambition, skillset, time invested, and relationships built. There are freight brokers that make $10,000 a year, and there are brokers that make millions of dollars a year. The opportunities are limitless!

The Skill Set of a High-Quality Freight Broker

Becoming a successful freight broker in the digital age is simple. It's not easy, but the steps are simple! A positive attitude can go along way as a freight broker in achieving success. You're dealing with people, and people have attitudes, bad days, issues at home, delays, mechanical breakdowns, etc. All these things can come to your front door simply because you interact with people daily. There's also the sales component, and with any sales job, you'll need to deal with a lot of No's to get to those lucrative Yes's.

After being in sales for several years, I realized that the skills required in sales are similar to the skills needed in several aspects of life. Up to and including dating, relationships, fitness, sports, etc. Here are nine critical competencies of freight brokers:

#1: Ability To Broaden Innovative Techniques:

A creative approach is a huge part of making your freight organization successful. There are unlimited links that make up a delivery chain. You need to be able to implement creative strategies to grow your business. As I stated earlier, dozens of factors come into play when engaging in moving freight from point A to point B. Successfully navigating these factors is the reason why freight brokerage is such a lucrative undertaking. Effectively managing these events takes creative planning and strategies.

#2: Ability To Hold Yourself Accountable and Organized:

Just like any business, when you work independently, you're your assistant, scheduler, booker, strategist, and financial planner. You cannot compete in this industry if you juggle all these roles.

Your organizational skills are one of the critical things that set you apart from other brokers. Even if you have no employees and do it all by yourself, you should present your customers' professional presence. Exceptional organizational skills will help you offer first-class customer support, as well as help you stay prepared for federal audits. In contrast, organization is an integral part of all businesses. Lack of organization in the logistics industry can put you out of business in the logistics industry.

#3: Effective Management of Workload & Personnel
Successful freight brokers must manage their workload, client expectations, and the output of their clients. As a broker, your client is your shippers, as well as your carriers.

You must ensure that your shippers:
    Have freight ready to be picked up on time
    Have freight ready to be unloaded on time
    Freight loaded/unloaded in a reasonable time frame
    Pay for the transportation of freight promptly
    Keep a professional demeanor with carriers

You must ensure carriers:

Pick-up freight on time

Deliver freight on time

Keep you up to date when delays occur

Keep a professional demeanor with shippers

You should be able to understand how easy it can be to get overwhelmed. You must also negotiate rates that make sure all parties involved feel that it is a win-win situation.

Work management starts and ends with having the proper systems and people in place. Whether it's you on your own or you have employees who can handle the business's critical components, the ability to have the right people in the right roles will help you manage your business profitably and effectively.

#4: Ability To Connect With Customers & Companies

Competency tests help you figure out the natural talents, gifts, and preferred communication styles of your employees and customers. Strong people skills will help you relate to a variety of personality types. Your job as a freight broker is to assist your clients, customers, and companies, get the goals accomplished effectively and efficiently. Just like your organizational skills, your interpersonal skills are non-negotiable components to the viability of your organization.

#5: Potential To Construct And Develop Your business:
After you've become a freight broker, you will need to focus on building a thriving business that grows. This requires:

• Negotiating skills – as stated earlier, assessing the appropriate rate to charge shippers and pay carriers while keeping a profit that makes it worthwhile to stay in business takes skill.

• Financial making plans – proper planning and a budget for long term success will go a long way in promoting business growth.

• Advertising and marketing – An effective marketing strategy is crucial in getting your name out there. The digital era allows for affordable marketing via the internet, social media channels, and online communities.

Just like any business, successful freight brokers are continually adding new skills to their repertoire. If you lack a particular ability, there are countless options to gain just about any skill. Here are a few options:

> YouTube
> Google
> Courses
> Industry Organizations
> Online Community Boards

#6: Networking

Gathering your list of clients and contacts may require strong networking skills. As you are connecting, you have to be strategic. Think about contacts that could help you connect with people in the logistics industry. This would be an excellent time to take out a piece of paper and list all the people you know. List everyone, because you never know who somebody knows.

Having business-to-business connections with other freight brokers is a major key to unlocking your business's potential through networking.

#7: Multi-Tasking

All brokers must have the ability to handle many tasks at once. Part of the day, you're connecting with clients. Then you're processing invoices and contacting vendors. You'll also communicate with carriers getting an ETA (Estimated Time of Arrival) for freight in transit. Issues such as weather, traffic, and mechanical breakdowns; can cause unforeseen delays. That requires you to contact the shipper; to keep them informed.

#8: Determining The Best Routes:

As a broker, your customers rely on you to determine the best options for getting the product from point A to point B with the fewest number of incidents. Technology has made this task so much easier. But technology can only provide you with real-time information. You have to do your research and make the right decisions. Proper planning a non-negotiable as a freight broker.

#9: Ensure Compliance

Every state, city, and municipality has its policies and guidelines for hauling freight. There are regulations on the federal level as well. These requirements are the reason that keeping your paperwork in order a must.

Chapter 2: Requirements For Freight Brokers

Now that you're acquainted with the essential roles of being a freight broker. It's time to look at the legal aspects of being a freight broker. Before you get started, you need to get your freight brokerage authority from the FMCSA (Federal Motor Carrier Safety Administration). This is what the industry calls getting your "numbers."

You must first get licensed with FMCSA's website: **fmcsa**.dot.gov. This is also where you'll pay the processing fee. As of this writing, the cost of this processing fee is $300.

Sidebar: You can hire a company to process your brokerage application or do it yourself. The process is simple, but some people feel more comfortable. Having a company do it for them.

The FMCSA has recently changed the licensing rules for freight brokers, motor carriers, and freight forwarders. Here are the basic requirements for registering your authority with the FMCSA:

- Designation of Process Broker – evidence of a BOC-3. This registration is required so that individuals, companies, attorneys, or the government. Have a physical address to serve you in the unfortunate event you're party to a lawsuit.

- Evidence of Financial Duty – this is the surety bond you'll need in the case of freight damage or loss. A BMC-84 Surety Bond of $75,000 is required

The FMCSA approval procedure can take as long as four to six weeks, but I've seen it done much quicker.

Fees to Get Started

The processing fees for becoming a freight broker vary depending on who processes your paperwork. If you do the paperwork yourself, it will be a lot cheaper. You'll only have to pay the federal processing fees.

Licensing and Registration expenses

As stated earlier, the first step in starting your career as a freight broker begins with registering with the Federal Motor Carrier Safety Administration, or FMCSA. They operate in conjunction with the US Department Of Transportation (DOT). They implement and monitor effective safety regulations for the motor carriers and the logistics industry as a whole. Registering with the FMCSA includes completing a form and paying a one-time, non-refundable fee of $300.

Furthermore, registering as a freight broker may also require additional licenses. Requirements can vary from state to state. So it's best to check with your local Secretary of State to avoid any unforeseen issues.

Surety Bond fees

All freight brokers need a surety bond as part of the licensing process. A surety bond acts as an assurance that goes into effect if you default on a carrier's payment or loss/damage to the freight. All freight brokers need to have a bond of at least $75,000 (but possibly more), ranging from 1 and 12% of the total bond amount, or $750 to $9,000. The cost of the bond depends on your credit score. The higher the credit score, the lower you have to pay for the bond.

Office Expense & Systems

Freight brokers need minimal home office equipment to get started. Such as:

➢ A computer
➢ A cellphone
➢ Internet connection

> ➢ A small place to work

Most new freight brokers work at home to save money. Others may use virtual office space instead of securing a conventional space. I prefer a laptop because it allows you to work virtually anywhere that you have an internet connection. As you can see, you can operate a brokerage on a shoestring budget!

Business Insurance

Regardless of the business, most proprietors confuse a surety bond with insurance. A surety bond ensures carriers are paid in the event you default on your obligations! Business coverage might also encompass liability coverage, asset insurance, and revenue insurance.

Software Prices

To compete in this industry, you must stay up to date on technological advancements. The speed of communication and executing tasks is essential in this industry. Loads that have the highest pay rate don't stay available for long. You'll have to know your numbers and expenses to know if a load is a good load before good opportunities come your way.

Many industry professionals are leaning on software solutions to help execute their daily tasks. Freight brokerage software may additionally consist of a Client Retention Management (CRM), a freight management software, or a transportation control software program. These tools increase your brokerage's performance.

Marketing & Advertising Costs

Established freight brokers can rely on word of mouth recommendations and referrals. For new brokers, buying advertising and marketing may be required. Fortunately, the digital age makes it cheaper to reach the masses. Growing a social media presence can help you create a community that looks at you as the industry leader. This is more of a long term strategy, but I would focus on it from the beginning.

Other outlets such as load board to generate leads, traditional advertising, marketing, social media, the internet, or attending networking occasions are the tools at your marketing disposal. The devices come at a cost. Do your research and pay attention to what works and what doesn't.

Different fees of operating as a Freight broker

As a freight broker, you may need to outsource specific tasks, such as paying a bookkeeper to track your revenue and expenses. A bookkeeper's fee can range from a few hundred bucks to a few thousand dollars. Also, deciding to buy additional tools such as business cards, a dedicated domain with business email, and a reliable internet connection.

The fees of becoming a broker can range from $4,000 to as much as $14,000. Thankfully, not all of these fees are reoccurring. There are a handful of fees you'll want to plan for annually. Those include your surety bond renewal, insurance renewals, ongoing software program fees, and expenses inclusive of advertising or office equipment.

Manage Expenses

Although the expense of becoming a freight broker is relatively low as compared to other start-up companies, the initial costs may be intimidating. If taking cash from your savings isn't an alternative for buying starting a freight brokerage profession, then other options exist. A business loan, personal mortgage, or a line of credit can be a simple way to finance the start-up process. It is essential to recognize that these methods come at a cost. Interest on the money borrowed should be added to your expenses; remember taking out a loan incurs risk. If the business fails, not only do you have to deal with the blow of closing a business. You'll also have to look at repaying the debt of a defunct company.

If some of these costs scare you, you may want to consider ways to cut certain costs. Instead of buying a new laptop, you can consider buying a used laptop, as well as other ways to cut costs without being cheap. Work on improving your credit score so that you can get a more affordable surety bond. Or you can get a co-signer for the surety bond.

These small steps can go a long way in making your freight brokerage profitable sooner rather than later. Also, make sure you have reserves to handle your living expenses as you grow your business. Many new brokers start part-time. This may be the best option for you. I've started businesses without reserves, with reserves, and while working another job or business. In my opinion, it's best to start a business while you have another job that takes care of your living expenses.

Kinds of insurance

As a freight broker, you need to carry all the necessary insurances that cover the cargo you haul and the different freight types you move. For example, if you have an insurance policy that doesn't allow you to carry alcohol. If you get a load containing alcohol, you'll need to get insurance for that specific load.

Types of Commercial Trucking Insurance

This section is for carriers who also choose to be freight brokers and vice versa. If that's not your goal, then you can bypass this section.

Commercial truck insurance is coverage that protects you in the event of loss or damage to equipment.

Primary Liability

Trucking coverage regulations begin with basic liability coverage for damage you may cause to other equipment or property.

As the name implies, it ensures that you meet minimum federal guidelines for coverage for all trucks and trailers, including leased units.

Physical damage coverage will cover for a commercial truck or trailer maintenance from damages like:

- ➤   Vandalism
- ➤   Collision
- ➤   Theft
- ➤   Acts of God – storms, earthquakes, etc.

Bobtail Coverage

Bobtail coverage is insurance for circumstances in which the truck doesn't have a trailer attached to it.

Cargo Insurance

This insurance is for coverage if something happens when the truck is attached to a trailer or hauling freight. This covers you in the event of loss of the cargo your hauling

Trailer Interchange

This coverage ensures all trailers that you may pull in the movement of freight. It is common for carriers to haul multiple leased trailers each day, leading to hundreds or even thousands of trailers during the year. So that you don't have to ensure each trailer you pull. Interchange insurance keeps you covered.

Uninsured/Underinsured Motorists

This insurance will protect you if another person hits you and doesn't have liability coverage.

Reefer Breakdown coverage

When you haul refrigerated trailers that maintain a specific temperature for temperature-sensitive freight such as frozen foods, reefer coverage will kick in.

Always look at insurance as an investment against worst-case scenarios. It's also vital that you're not underinsured. I remember getting into an accident and losing my truck. The truck was insured for the amount that I paid for it, which would only cover the balance that I owed the bank. But I would be out a truck. The truck value was twice that of the amount owed. Had I had proper insurance, I could've paid my loan off and bought a new truck. The truck was eventually repaired, but it was never the same after the accident. The minor mistake caused a significant setback in my business.

More About The Surety Bond

As stated earlier, a surety bond is to initiate or renew your authority; it establishes credibility so that carriers and shippers feel more comfortable working with you.

How Much Does It Cost?

The Federal Motor Carrier Safety Association (FMCSA) requires a surety bond of $75,000. Luckily, you don't have to pay the entire amount upfront, depending on your credit rating. You pay a fraction of that amount (usually between 1% and 12%). This is an annual fee

Shippers work with freight forwarders who negotiate contracts on behalf of shippers to ensure that they're accountable for any issues while freight is in transit. Cargo coverage comes in handy a shipper refuses to accept a shipment.

Freight brokers and forwarders are not required to carry cargo insurance, but companies are reluctant to work with companies that aren't insured. Because they know if there's any damage or the carrier refuses the entire delivery, the shipper will contact the freight forwarder to process the claim.

Importance of Performance History For Freight Brokers

The industry has a system of checks and balances; when a carrier, shipper, or broker fails to fulfill their obligations, the aggrieved party will report their lack of follow-thru to the appropriate reporting agency.

- The shipper will report broker performance on the handling of their load. As more shippers negatively report a broker, the harder it'll be for the broker to work with shippers. This will also affect how much shippers are willing to pay a broker

- The brokers report data about payment patterns of shippers. Shippers who are slow to pay will eventually run out of brokers and carriers to work with them

- Brokers and shippers report data about the performance history of carriers. In turn, carriers report the payment history of shippers and brokers. As well if payments are in line with the original agreement.

Factoring Companies

These are financial intermediaries that provide loans to carriers. These loans bridge the gap between when a carrier transports the load and when the shipper pays the carrier. These are vital logistics industry members, as many carriers can't afford to wait for the usual 30 to 90 days it takes to secure payment from the shipper.

The factoring company will review the shipper's payment history before approving payment to a carrier.

Freight Broker Seasoning

As a new freight broker, you'll go through an arbitrary probationary period; because the established companies don't know your performance history. All brokerages are graded depending on the time in business and growth. It takes on average six months to a year to establish relationships and credibility with shippers and carriers. This is referred to as your book of business.

By now, you can see that becoming a freight broker requires little to no cost upfront. But it requires a lot of hard work and perseverance to become established. Maintaining a persistent attitude and a positive outlook in the face of conre is a skill. This is why we suggest having reserves to make sure the bills are paid during these difficult times.

Importance of Cargo Insurance

A 2017 survey of shippers discovered that their primary complaint is damage to cargo. Eventually, all shippers and carriers run into issues with damaged freight. What's worse is that most people can't afford to pay for damaged cargo.

Cargo insurance protects the freight and reduces the monetary risk of all goods which might be damaged in transit. Each broker must maintain a minimal amount of cargo insurance.

Cargo Insurance Limitations

Unfortunately, no cargo insurance covers all instances. The Carmack Amendment of 1906 limits coverage to loss or damage of property. The shipper is only required to make sure the cargo is shipped in good condition. The carrier is then wholly responsible for the shipment. Additionally, a certificate of coverage does not necessarily mean that the broker's claim will be covered by way of the stated insurance.

Types Of Cargo Insurance

Cargo Insurance has variations for domestic and international freight and variations depending on the form of transportation. They're grouped into following classes of shipment coverage:

Ground Shipment Insurance

Ground shipment insurance covers robbery, damages, and a number of different risks. The insurance is the most common insurance used, and it covers trucks and trailers from coast to coast

Importance Of Cargo Insurance

It's crucial to purchase cargo insurance; loads are transported on a global vessel, which exposes them to different dangers. Numerous issues can cause freight to be lost or damaged. Here we'll look at a few:

Containers Lost At Sea

That sounds far-fetched, but approximately 733 bins get lost at sea every year. That's only counting boxes lost and no longer includes the hurt or perished people on the vessel.

Cargo damage

Goods can get damaged in transit. There are specific steps shippers should take to reduce the likelihood of damage to goods, such as securing the cargo. But the risk still remains

Significance of a Strong Corporate Presence

Most successful freight brokers are great at communication, customer service skills, and healthy relationships.

As a broker, you're an independent contractor to focus on a region with lots of freight running in and out of it. The digital age allows you to have a presence in various regions.

If you are an aspiring broker, it may be a good idea to get an apprenticeship with an existing broker; until you have your book of business. This helps you create relationships. An established brokerage firm will ensure that you have access to superior equipment, technology, and a supportive office.

A freight dealer with credibility will assure your clients that their cargo is in safe hands, and they'll tend to trust you more, which will lead to more business.

Coping With Price Fluctuations

Over time, you should be able to pay carriers before you receive payment from the shipper. A line of credit would be a great asset for such a significant outlay of cash. This helps because some carriers don't work with factoring companies but would appreciate a brokerage that pays them in a timely fashion.

The bottom line for any successful broking is to ensure that you have proper certifications, keep detailed documentation, enough insurance coverage, and substantial liquid assets. Otherwise, you'll struggle to get carriers and shippers to work with you consistently.

Due Diligence

As a broker, you want to gather all the information you can about shippers and carriers. You'll also want to supply carriers with a broker packet that gives the carrier detailed information about your company.

This packet will help your carriers get an understanding of rates and payment schedules. In a nutshell, like any business, organization, and professionalism will go a long way.

Advertising, Marketing, and Networking

Once your business is up and running, you'll need to begin advertising, marketing, and networking to put your name in front of potential shippers and carriers. There are many approaches to marketing your company. Offer services and benefits that your competitors fail to offer. One benefit is brokering freight in locations where others aren't. For example, carriers usually struggle to find loads pulling out of Florida. A broker who has a steady amount of freight in Florida would stand out from the crowd.

There are countless options to market your business, including sales, advertising, marketing, and networking. Such as:

➢ Reaching out to shippers & carriers expand your database Using social media ads to promote your business

➢ Emailing campaigns to people you already know

➢ A social media business page (a digital business card)

➢ Ads in trade magazines

➢ A high-quality business website.

Therefore, take the time to craft your digital footprint. Your website and social media pages should be informative and user-friendly. It should give people a reason to contact you as it clearly defines your brand and states that you are a freight brokerage company.

To be a successful freight broker, you must consistently focus on growing a customer base or business book. Having a solid book of business will help you make better business decisions; you lose a shipper or carrier in the event. In my experience, we often cut corners or work with people we'd rather not because we have limited options. That's we must make it a daily habit to prospect for new business. This is especially true if you have one or two clients who bring in the bulk of your business. Let's say you have five shippers that provide you with freight; luckily for you, a handful of shippers provide enough cargo to make your business profitable and provide you with an excellent quality of life. But 2 of those shippers account for 75% of your revenue. On Monday, the owner of one of those companies retires and sells their business. The new owner already has a broker they work with and decides to cut ties with you. Then on Wednesday, you have a falling out with the other shipper, and they decide to cut ties with you. Now 75% of your business and income is gone in a matter of days. Lack of diversity could put you out of business before the end of the month. Consistent prospecting, networking, marketing, and advertising would be a proactive step in preventing its effects on your business.

As freight brokers, you do not transport freight, your serve as a connector between shippers and carriers. Your most significant assets are knowledge, communication, and people skills. Ultimately, you connect dependable shippers with dependable carriers.

Chapter 3: Working with Customers

If this is your first attempt into a service-based business, you may think you want to work with as many clients as possible on the surface, that sounds great. However, experience has taught me that not all clients are good for business. It's sort of like dating. We've all had horrible first dates. When this happens, we usually never see that person again. But with business, we have a terrible initial interaction with a client, and because of that dangling carrot of money, we ignore the red flags of unreasonable clients. It's important to remember that each prospect is a human being, and just like we don't get along with everyone, we will not get along with every candidate. Here are a few strategies for dealing with customers.

Strategy 1: Don't Work With Unreliable Clients

For the most part, there are two types of customers. Customers who can be slow but reliable are usually huge businesses that insist on paying invoices on net-25 to net-60 day terms. Meaning you get paid 25 to 60 days after the freight is delivered. They can be remarkable customers and provide a steady stream of income. Making it well worth it to accept these terms, the only issue is while you wait for them to pay, you still have bills to pay. This delay can put you out of business. In this instance, the best solution is to use a factoring company to bridge the gap between delivery and payment

On the other hand, you have slow and unreliable customers, and they come in all shapes and sizes. They wait the maximum allotment of time to pay, and sometimes they never pay. A factoring company comes in handy here because they will refuse to pay an advance if you work with this type of customer. However, this only works if you contact the factoring company BEFORE you work with the shipper.

You can also do your research on the payment history of anyone that you work with. As a freight broker, you extend credit to any shipper you work with, similar to a bank. If your research tells you that a particular shipper is a high risk, you may request a partial or full charge in advance. However, it might be best not to work with this type of client altogether. Back to the dating analogy, you have to notice the red flags, and it will save you a lot of headaches in the future.

If you see yourself working with a difficult client, the longer a company goes without paying an invoice, the less likely they'll pay that invoice. Make sure to follow up on any past due invoices quickly and with courtesy, and don't forget to consult with an attorney after the agreed up payment period expires.

Strategy # 2: Expedited Payment Terms

Some shippers will agree to expedited payment terms, a shorter due date than the usual 30 to 60 days. Shippers generally agree to quick pay if the broking can provide them a rate reduction for expedited payments. Expedited payments can help when getting starting or during lean times. One of my income streams, involves social media management. I charge a standard rate for promotions, but I will reach out to people who previously inquired about promotions during a cash crunch and offered a reduced rate. Major corporations do this, as well. This is why companies offer end of season and end of year promotions. This is the same reason for clearance racks in your local clothing store.

Approach 3: Freight Factoring

Freight factoring sounds complicated, but it's relatively simple. Factoring is the process of selling your receivables to a third party. In most instances, you're paid 70-95% of the invoice within a matter of days. After the factoring agency gets your receivable balance, you'll receive your full compensation, minus the factoring company's profit. Expenses can range between 1 to 5% of the total invoice.

While 1.5% doesn't appear to be a lot, but if you use factoring all of the time, those fees can add up.

Another fundamental problem is whether or not your factoring association is non-ration or ration. When you component on a ration basis, if the shipper doesn't pay the receivable, the factoring company goes back to the broker. In this case, the broker is liable for non-payment. This is why it's essential to research the shippers that you work with. In non-ration situations, if the shipper doesn't pay the receivable, the factoring company takes on the loss.

Factoring can offer temporary relief to help with payables and help you keep your business going.

Factoring is relatively common in the logistics industry. As with every industry, a few will be straightforward about their fees and schedule of payments, while others will now not. It's vital to thoroughly vet any factoring company, just as you'd vet any lender or purchaser.

Approach 4: Concise & Regular Communication

A crucial element to creating a successful freight brokerage is consistent communication. Many individuals have formed multiple brokerages simply to shut down after pocketing earnings without paying their clients. They're initially legitimate organizations and get customers to give them larger and larger accounts. They eventually get repeat business, but then they begin to slow pay or no longer pay at all. They eventually shut down and tend to return in a year or so. In a brand new location, with a new number and start the technique all over again.

Bad apples like this affect the entire industry. This is why brokers must communicate regularly with their clients. As well as thoroughly vetting any employees before hiring them. Employees that have access to your database of shippers and carriers can do a world of damage to your credibility.

Cash flow management is vital in any business. As a broker, you'll have expenses going out before receivables come in. Techniques like factoring and short pay arrangements can help with these difficulties.

Full-service brokers also offer clients cash management services to forecast revenue, leading to a funding strategy. Full-service brokers do enough market studies and meet with enough people; their fee is between $100 and $200 per client.

Similar to commissions, brokers have maintenance and operating expenses. Some brokers have inactivity fees; if a carrier goes months without moving any freight.

Types Of FREIGHT

There are a myriad of freight options; we'll take

1. Less Than Truckload Freight

Less than truckload (LTL) is in high demand because it pays well, requires a dependable carrier, and the freight is time-sensitive. LTL carriers get higher priority at shippers as well. It's a cost-effective approach to transporting smaller loads. LTL shipping offers room for different shippers to group other shippers on a single load.

2. Full Truckload Freight

Full truckload (FTL) freight uses the entire space and weight capacity of the trailer. These loads are for shippers that have more freight to transfer. Your major shippers such as Target, Walmart, and Amazon pay a premium for this service, but their shipment is delivered within their time frame.

3. Intermodal Rail Freight

Intermodal rail freight delivery is a lucrative undertaking as well. Freight is picked up at a warehouse in a hub city or surrounding suburb such as Atlanta, Chicago, Los Angeles, etc., delivered to a local rail yards cross-country on a train. These freight trains are what hold up your morning commute when you're stuck at a railroad crossing. Then picked up in a connecting city, and a new driver in that city delivers the load. Watching trailers get loaded and unloaded from a train is a cool experience for anyone who ever played with trucks as a child. This saves the shipper money as the freight is usually double stacked and more compact on the train. The train also avoids such delays as traffic, weather, and HOS constraints. Canadian rail lines also connect to this massive network.

4. AIR FREIGHT

The fastest freight way to deliver your cargo is through the use of air freight. Airfreight companies are committed to coping with the logistics for transporting smaller packages. Even as air freight is costly compared to other transportation modes, it's the first-class alternative for delivery time-specific and urgent shipments.

5. OCEAN FREIGHT

The primary solution for transport freight around the world is to use ocean freight. Cargo shipped via boat offers some of the most effective strategies.

6. EXPEDITED FREIGHT

Expedited freight is also referred to as hotshot loads, and it allows for different freight types to be transported at a premium. Hotshot loads are often transported with pick-up trucks

Dispatchers

The trucking industry relies on dependable drivers to transport freight in a safe and timely manner. Dispatchers play a critical position, as well. A dispatcher creates the timetable for the pick-up and delivery of cargo.

Truck dispatchers have the following duties:

- Dispatchers retain information by monitoring drivers' movements. Checking for violations of regulations and monitoring their hours and availability.

- They keep track of the capacity of a particular truckload

- they're a dependable intermediary between drivers, brokers, and shippers

- they determine routes and timelines to move freight in a safe and efficient manner
- they determine strategies and negotiate rates directly with carriers and customers.

Types Of Freight Broker

Asset-Based Brokers

Asset-based freight brokers have their freight to transport—the house freight in warehouses, distribution centers, or trucks. Asset-based brokers rarely have all of the tools required to move or store freight. They work directly with shippers to coordinate the transportation of the products.

Non-Asset based Freight brokers

Non-asset based freight broker do not own the freight that they are responsible for transporting. They have the responsibility of working with shippers and carriers. They work with a network of shippers to transfer cargo to the right location. A non-asset based freight brokers supply the shipper with a point of contact throughout the delivery process. Generally, freight brokers have relationships with carriers that they entrust to move freight.

Non-asset based freight brokers are thought to have no direct gateway to trucks, trailers, and drivers; which isn't true. Most non-asset based freight brokers have direct access to countless numbers of trucks. They work with a variety of companies and carriers to get goods from point A to point B. In some instances, non-asset based freight brokers have access to more trucks than an asset-based freight broker depending on their provider community's dimensions.

Freight Broker Ratings

While most freight brokerages are trustworthy businesses that practice ethical standards, it's essential for carriers to professionally deal with brokers. Unfortunately, freight brokers make delayed payments, which constitutes a significant threat to companies.

Building Credibility As A Brand New Broker

Beginning a new freight brokerage is a brutal act. Even if you have years of personal experience with customers, freight management, and trucking companies. You can have trouble getting shippers, carriers, and factoring companies to work with you. The industry looks at it as giving a teenager keys to a sports car. That inherent risk is the reason insurance companies charge new drivers high premiums. And just like a teenage driver, new brokers are deemed high risk.

When a new broker attempts to work with a carrier, the carrier does their research to decide whether they'll work with a broker. This is to determine the payment history of the broker. This is why freight brokers have to start slow and gradually build their credibility over time.

A carrier's offering can be lost in the sea of competition, especially for busier lanes. How can a broker make that load stand out? Displaying a competitive rate will help; however, carriers prefer to work with established companies. But how do brokers establish credibility?

Here are five recommendations to assist in building credibility as a new broker:

1. Send payments electronically – The digital age has made instant payment options a must. Carriers expect to get paid in the most efficient manner possible!

2. Make payments electronically – Using EFT's to make payments to vendors expedite matters and gives your vendors the confidence to make your brokerage a priority. Furthermore, in the event of a cash shortage, the vendor is more likely to extend credit.

3. Checking Email regularly and snail mail each day – placing alerts on emails from certain vendors or clients mark those messages as a higher priority. It ensures that they don't get lost in a sea of mundane emails. The postal service also offers alerts so that you get notified when specific packages or letters are delivered.

4. Tracking missing or delayed messages or deliveries. – When you don't receive an important email or something from a carrier in a timely way, start researching its whereabouts.

5. Constantly growing your business - always have the long term view; customer acquisition is the most time consuming and expensive part of any business. Take good care of your current clients and always prospect for new clients.

Broker's Credit Reporting Agencies
Ansonia is a credit reporting agency that measures an organization's creditworthiness. It is based on the number of days the broker takes to pay an invoice, outstanding collection accounts, history of collection accounts, and bankruptcies. A credit score of 87 and above is considered low risk, while credit scores below 70 are seen as high risk

Carriers 411

Carrier411 is the logistics industries leading provider when it comes to monitoring companies. It helps brokers and shippers make important decisions by assessing the risk associated with working with certain carriers. They keep track of safety ratings, SMS simple rankings, and different vital statistics about carriers. They confirm provider compliance and streamline the onboarding process of carriers. This allows companies to vet trucking companies in seconds.

This system allows you to choose the carriers you want to keep an eye on, upload them to your list of carries that you observe. The tracking software then notifies you when modifications occur. You're provided with custom service reviews and the use of a Qualification Record Card to assess the safety ratings of all vendors. As mentioned earlier, you get access to SMS simple scores, history of insurance claims, vital information about their operating authority, out of service claims, and FreightGuard reports.

Chapter 4: Prospecting For Shippers Carriers & Freight

Prospecting for shippers and carriers is the most challenging job that freight brokers face. But this is also the lifeblood of your business.

With so much competition trying to undercut rates, it makes turning a profit on loads more and more difficult. That is why you must separate your brokerage from the rest. So that clients continue to work with you, and potential clients choose to work with you. Here are a few tips for navigating this competitive landscape:

1. Focus On Warm Prospects First

Consistently interacting with people you've already worked with can assist you in building relationships with shippers. This can be family members, friends, or former co-workers. This is powerful because regardless of the industry, people do business with people they know, like, and trust. All things being equal, people tend to do business with being friends. Even when someone outside of your circle of influence can provide better service, people still tend to do business with a friend.

Pinpoint the people in a high position at the logistics division of their employer. These roles include Logistics Coordinator, Procurement Analyst, consumer/purchasing, transport professional, deliver Chain Manager, Operations Manager.

Individuals in these positions will frequently be involved with transferring shipments for their respective employers and help you get your foot in the door with decision-makers.

2. Pay Attention To Your Local Environment

Keep a close eye on the industrial parks and warehouses in your vicinity. Once you locate these operations, start studying what kind of freight they manufacture or transport, their requirements, what lanes they run, and who is the decision-maker when it comes to supply chain management. Driving around these areas, combined with a little legwork and the internet, can make you familiar with a room within a matter of weeks.

When you are making contact with the decision-makers, qualify them by finding out where they are having problems in their supply chain. Don't allow them to persuade you that there are not any gaps in their supply chain. This may be true on the surface. But any seasoned salesperson knows how to find the pain points of any prospect.

Every shipper deals with a shipment delivered late or has had bad experiences with customer service. It's your job to find these gaps; with consistency and hard work, you should get the clients to open up about competitor shortcomings.
It is then your job to show the prospect how your company can fill those gaps.

3. The Power of The Internet
As with any business, the internet provides the opportunity for unlimited information about competitors, prospects, and clients.

4. Become An Expert With A Niche Commodity
Many companies are successful because they don't try and be everything to everybody. They choose to find a specific niche to focus on and become the best provider available in that niche. The saying goes, don't dig a hole a foot deep and a mile wide; dig a hole a foot wide and a mile deep. Find your sweet spot in the industry and dominate it.
Customers admire companies that have experience hauling specific freight and running lanes that they need to be managed.

This experience can make you an expert in the niche, allowing you to command higher rates.

Customers will pay a premium for service that tailors to their needs; they will pay a bit extra to ship with you, understanding that their freight is in good hands. By focusing on a specific niche, you'll have relationships with carriers who run freight in your niche.

The easier you make this process, the more likely they will work with your organization. People pay a premium for convenience. That is why companies such as Uber and DoorDash have grown over the years. For example, you'll pay a higher price for the same product at your local drug store to avoid waiting in long lines in a supermarket.

5. Generate Referrals

The most profitable and easiest way to generate new business is through the referrals of friends, family members, or clients. Before you can get a referral, you have to provide excellent service and ask for a referral. Periodically, customers will refer you to their colleagues.

6. Social Media

Social media puts billions of people at your fingertips at any given time. The platforms are underutilized in the logistics industry. Most companies describe their business basics in their profile; you can direct message them to start a relationship and find out how your business can be of service to them. Many companies have created dynamic social media accounts with massive outreach to manage client relationships and enhance engagement with their audience.

7. Go Door-to-Door

The traditional method of walking up to a prospect's business, introducing yourself, and establishing a relationship is a time tested method. This method isn't for the faint of heart as you'll be facing constant rejection; however, the goal is to get in contact with the decision-maker.

This is when your broker packet will come in handy. Even if you can't get a prospect to work with you on the initial sales call, they may be a great candidate to follow up with in the future.

9. Get Familiar With Other Customers in Your Existing Lanes

Suppose you're already making deliveries to a particular area. Finding other customers who ship out of that area can provide a win-win for all parties involved. Since the load and carrier are already in the area, they can serve another client in that city or town at a more affordable rate. Carriers love to have a steady supply of freight because they only make money when their wheels are moving.

As discusses earlier, customer service is the best way to get referral business. It's just as critical when it comes to client retention. Finding a client who is easy to work with and has enough freight for you to haul; is a huge undertaking once you have reached an agreement with someone you want to provide that client with white glove customer service.

Prospecting For Clients

1. Get connected.

The easiest method to finding new business is to invite different freight brokers to refer you to providers. Join a company that's apart of the Transportation Intermediaries Association (TIA). TIA is a freight broker's network that may create connections, access freight, and continue education on crucial logistics topics. Members of TIA have access to lists of qualified drivers and use of the TIA Watchdog database. It allows contributors to notify one another of fraudulent operators. Users can report illegal re-brokering of shipments, no-shows, cancellations, theft, unethical loss of freight, and other issues.

2. Pay Premium Prices

Generally, low paying freight attracts lower quality carriers, and high-paying freight appeals to high-quality carriers. Make sure to understand competitive rates pay carriers a price consistent with the marketplace.

You can get an idea of industry rates by researching load boards. Load boards are like eBay, Amazon, or Craigslist for available freight; you can access these through an app. While these boards aren't free, it's a good investment to pay for their services. A load board is a platform wherein trucking organizations link with freight brokers and shippers.

Although some of the trucking load forums are connected to use, others require a monthly payment. The wrong side is that there can be tight competition, and not all loads are profitable. Use Load boards as a way to season your brokerage. Make use of multiple load boardzl so one can discover the exceptional offers.

Another method to attract reliable carriers is to be a dependable and responsible broker. Treat carriers the same way that you want to be treated. Pay vendors on time, communicate regularly.

It's essential to know the trucking business's regulations and policies, such as Hours of service (HOS) guidelines. FMCSA sets these guidelines to limit how long drivers can be on the road. They have strict limits on rest breaks, the number of hours you can be on-duty, and the numbers of hours drivers can drive in a day. These regulations ensure the safety of drivers, passengers, and other vehicles. Set realistic expectations for your clients as to the timeframe of delivers and pick-ups. It's important to remember all the variables that come into play in the logistics industry.

Exceptional Shippers/Carriers Attracted Exceptional Brokers who pay them well and pay responsibly.

The bidding procedure for brokers
Proudly owning a truck business comes with many challenges. And finding profitable freight and dependable carriers takes work. As an entrepreneur, customer service and marketing will help you find a steady supply of loyal shippers and loyal carriers.

Nearby agencies

Connect with neighborhood grocery stores, producers, puppy food vendors, etc. Prospect for new clients, calling possible leads, distribute fliers, and communicate to their delivery departments.

Properly Negotiating Rates

There is a lot of techniques available that assist you in having the ability to negotiate your pay, which includes:

knowing the specifics needs of prospects

learn everything you can about those needs

positive feedback

Rates listed on load boards usually have hidden fees; uncover these by being very cautious when accepting a load. More often than not, these rates can be negotiated.

Using Load Boards

Load boards typically determine the average price for a specific load.

The longer a load spends on a load board, the less likely it will be chosen by a carrier. This can be an opportunity to flex your negotiating skills.

Some lanes are more challenging to operate than others. This is where you can discover if there are any tolls alongside your route. Do you need special approval to transport specific freight into certain locations? Find out if you'll get compensated for lengthy wait times (Otherwise known as detention). There are countless load boards that carriers peruse to find suitable carriers to haul their freight.

Get the whole lot in writing

Before you pick-up, any load, make sure you know precisely how much you'll be compensated, which is called a rate con (confirmation). It's an agreement between two or more parties on freight delivery in a specific time frame for a specific amount.

Verifying Broker and Shipper Information

Credit verification prevents you from working with unreputable chippers and carriers. You'll be able to have proof of their payment history.

Your First Year As A Freight Broker

In your first year of being a broker, you will face many demanding situations. This learning curve depends on your background, as well. It'll be a smoother transition if you've already been in the logistics industry. Here are some indicators that could make your first loads simpler.

1. With this being your first year as a freight broker, most companies won't feel comfortable working with you due to a lack of seasoning or a track record. Having carriers on hand at least gives you the credibility to get freight moved. In general, shippers are worried about trusting new brokers to move freight.

2.   Your credit score will determine your insurance and bond rates. As stated earlier, you'll have to pay for the first year of your bond. Having a solid credit score will drive down your costs. Conversely, a bad credit score will cause a higher rate.

3.   Factoring – once you've agreed with a shipper to move freight and a carrier to transport it, you're officially in business. However, the carrier is ready to get paid immediately, and you'll likely have an invoice without actual payment. A stable relationship with a factoring company beforehand will help make this crucial next step a smooth transition. Carriers who know you have a relationship with a credible factoring agency will be more likely to work with you.

After your first 12 months, you'll have an established history within the industry and become seasoned. Congratulations, many brokers don't make it to this all-important milestone. By now, you'll have a system of working with drivers, understand dispatching, delivery, factoring, and office management. You'll also focus on the high-quality tasks you excel at and delegate or outsource the rest.

Remember, No matter what you must always prospect for new business. Because, there will always be a competitor who is looking to take your clients, relationships and book of business from you. This is why you must provide excellent customer service, and stay in tune with your client's needs on a daily, weekly, and monthly basis. After working so hard to obtain new business it's even more important to maintain it.

Chapter 5: Should You Work With An Existing Freight Broker?

Working for a freight broker is easier and less expensive. It allows you to ride the learning curve on someone else's dime. You'll also have mentorship and leadership to help you along the way. This will also allow you to establish a book of business. The key is, will you be allowed to take that book of business with you upon your departure, or will there be a non-compete clause in your employment contract.

You would have the responsibility of brokering freight on behalf of your company. The intent is for a mutually beneficial business relationship that enables the broker to act under the company's authority. Conversely, the broker benefits from an increase in opportunities due to the credibility of a reputable brokerage. Broker may enter into employment or independent contractor agreements with their company, or their course of conduct with a particular company can create a fiduciary responsibility to their company.

When working with an existing broker, you'll spend most of your time and resources searching for and identifying new prospects. Any new customer that you find technically belongs to the broker.

The key is who has control of these new clients in the event you leave the company. The broker may require that if you leave the brokerage, you have a waiting period of several months before working with your current customers and carriers again. If the broker signs such an agreement, they are bound by its restrictions.

One of the most significant benefits of working with an existing broker is that you can work from home! This is appealing to thousands of professionals who don't want to come into an office. While getting your broker authority is relatively inexpensive to other business start-ups, getting the surety bond or trust fund is a problem if a person does not have good credit or has little or no credit history. By working for another company, you could avoid all these fees.

In general, you'll work early in the morning prospecting for shippers to haul their freight. When you're calling customers to get loads, the calls should be made earlier in the morning. When following up with your current clients, those calls should be made in the middle of the day. Typically, you'll have your evenings free; other than monitoring loads that are currently in-transit

As a broker, your business relies heavily on the logistics industry's overall health as a whole. There are barriers and obstacles that each broker needs to familiarize themselves with.

National fuel rates have a direct impact on rates as well. Damage to a pipeline in a particular area or political unrest in an oil supplier nation; has an immediate effect on your business. High fuel and other increased operating costs can put trucking companies out of business, which reduces your supply of carriers.

The Covid-19 pandemic was a great indicator of the strength of the logistics industry. So much so that it was labeled an essential business. Unfortunately, lower demand for freight caused shipping rates to go down. Which caused many carriers to park their trucks; this had a trickle-down effect on the entire industry. However, once areas opened back up, demand in the industry skyrocketed. Such volatility isn't commonplace in the industry. It does show the importance of logistics professionals staying in tune with global, national, and local trends.

Regardless of the industry's ups and downs, there will always be a demand for good brokers that can navigate freight movement across the globe. Furthermore, dependable brokers with a good track record will always have a steady flow of clients.

Most people who own freight brokerage companies decide to work with another brokerage to leave behind costly overhead, stress, and responsibilities that come from owning a freight brokerage company. That way, they'll be able to focus mainly on sales and operations and less on administrative duties. All while earning a fair amount of money.

The following are some reasons for running your brokerage can be a lot more stressful than working as a freight broker for a brokerage.

COSTLY OVERHEAD

Starting and maintaining a freight brokerage isn't necessarily expensive. But the ongoing operating expenses can add up. Start-up and operating costs for a new brokerage span from $3,000 to $15,000.

MASSIVE TIME INVESTMENT

A lot of time is put into establishing your own freight brokerage company. The ongoing expenses related to establishing a freight brokerage; lead to significant amounts of time expended organizing a wide variety of operations. Operating your brokerage also means "wearing many hats — especially in the back office, where tasks such as technology setup, carrier approval and setup, payables and receivables, and much more."

RISKS AND STRESS

People who can spare enough working hours and raise enough money to open a freight brokerage company should come to grips with the risks involved — not the least of which is cash flow. Paying carriers while you wait for shippers to pay you can be very stressful, primarily if you're operating on modest capital reserves. Even using a factoring company can be a liability because they do charge fees for their bridge loans. Brokers can lose tens of thousands and even hundreds of thousands of dollars with factoring companies.

An initial credit risk assessment is critical; consistently observing customer payment patterns is a must. It's a laborious, pain-staking process, but failure to do so could bring the whole business down.

Lawsuits are inevitable for brokers; you'll encounter claims, and it's essential to be prepared. Even then, lawsuits aren't fun, especially when they come in the infancy of your brokerage.

CHAPTER 6: Factors Affecting The Logistics Industry

FMCSA Revisions & Global Challenges

As a broker, you'll have to stay in tune with new rules and regulations on the federal, state, and local levels. Any changes will most likely affect the profitability of a freight brokerage. New government sanctions can affect your bottom line as well. Any time a US trade embargo is placed in effect with a particular country, it will directly affect the logistics industry as a whole. Events such as the Chinese New Year has a direct impact on the supply of freight every year.

Factors that affect Freight Rates

Rates for freight are influenced by many factors depending on the cargo being hauled, the time of year it's being transported, the demand for particular freight, the sensitive nature of specific loads, etc.

You'll also need to stay abreast of any tariffs or taxes that coincide with the freight you're shipping, depending on the policies of certain nations, countries, states, or municipalities. You could be on the hook for these fees.

Calculating freight pricing isn't an easy task.

Carriers negotiate rates based on commodity, value, equipment availability, volume, customer service factors, and payment history. As a broker, you need to know what these market variables are. It can also cause increases or decreases in the per-mile rate, such as driver shortages, fuel surcharges, seasonal changes, terrain, region, tolls, and so on. We mention region because some carriers are leery of driving in certain parts of the country. Such as New York City or certain parts of Colorado. At the time of this writing, the State of California has infinitely more restrictions than most US states. Many shippers—especially large companies with experienced traffic departments— determine how much they're willing to pay for a shipment. If this amount is unreasonable, you'll need to negotiate with the shipper or decline to handle the load.

Other factors that influence rates include:

The Labor Market For Commercial Drivers

The rise in wages and competition between carriers for competent drivers; has had an effect on expenses in the industry. While more drivers can lead to more bad drivers. Overall, you're more prone to select the better carriers because you have a larger pool to choose from in the selection process

Geopolitical events

International maritime shipping has become fraught with the dangers of pirates and rogue governments. In an estimate provided by the world bank, losses incurred from global piracy amounted to approximately $18 billion in 2014, forcing adjusting shipping routes and higher pay for insurance premiums.

Shipper's Reputation

A shipper's reputation is dependent on the carrier's expectations as to checking in with the shipper and unloading time. If the shipper has a reputation for loading quickly, such shippers may be charged discounted shipping rates. The industry is fraught with carriers who have spent hour if not days at a shipper waiting to get loaded or unloaded. As you know, carriers don't make money when their wheels aren't turning.

Check out Maurice's other books:

6 Figure Trucking: You're Only One Decision Away From $150K

6 Figure Teens: Earn Six Figures Before Your 21st Birthday

To help us continue to bring the best books to the market. Please leave a review on the platform that you bought this book about what you gained from reading these pages. This also gives new readers the opportunity to see what knowledge other readers gained from this book

Check out Maurice's other books:

6 Figure Trucking: You're Only One Decision Away From $150K

6 Figure Teens: Earn Six Figures Before Your 21st Birthday

6 Figure Entrepreneur: Start A Business That Nets Over $100k

To help us continue to bring the best books to the market. Please leave a review on the platform that you bought this book about what you gained from reading these pages. This also gives new readers the opportunity to see what knowledge other readers gained from this book. You can also visit mauricethe1st.com for other resources. If you'd like to take your life or business to the next level; contact Maurice personally at maurice@mauricethefirst.com

REFERENCES

https://www.invoicefactoring.com/factoring-blog/freight-brokers/fear-and-loathing-in-freight-brokering

https://www.tafs.com/negotiating-freight-rates

https://www.invoicefactoring.com/factoring-blog/freight-brokers/fear-and-loathing-in-freight-brokering

https://www.directfreight.com/blog/what-does-the-average-freight-broker-make/

https://www.jwsuretybonds.com/blog/how-much-does-it-cost-to-become-a-freight-broker

https://www.google.com/search?client=ms-opera-mini-iphone&channel=new&ei=NlqoX-acNoHKgQaBl7mQCg&q=skill+set+of+a+great+freight+broker&oq=skill+set+of+a+great+freigh-

https://www.brunswickcompanies.com/surety-bonds/license-and-permit-bond/freight-broker-bond/

https://www.brunswickcompanies.com/surety-bonds/license-and-permit-bond/freight-broker-bond

https://operfi.com/how-can-a-new-broker-build-credit-by-partnering-with-a-factoring-company/

https://www.dat.com/blog/post/5-simple-ways-brokers-can-improve-their-credit-score

https://www.carrier411.com/carrier-monitoring-service.cfm

https://www.invoicefactoring.com/factoring-blog/freight-brokers/3-tips-to-find-quality-carriers

https://www.ibm.com/support/knowledgecenter/SSFCZ3_10.6.0/com.ibm.tri.doc/proc_topics/c_bidding_process.html

https://www.indeed.com/cmp/Carrier/salaries

https://www.tafs.com/negotiating-freight-rates/

https://transportation.trimble.com/resources/blogs/mastering-the-freight-bidding-process-before-it-masters-you

https://bizfluent.com/how-6967282-bid-loads-trucking.html

https://www.merchantmaverick.com/understanding-commercial-truck-insurance/

https://freight-tec.com/2018/02/19/the-pros-and-cons-of-starting-a-freight-brokerage-company/

https://www.groundforcelogistics.com/6-benefits-of-using-a-freight-broker/

Working as a Broker in the Transportation Industry By John D. Thomas
http://atexfreightbrokertraining.com/ba-trng/

Made in the USA
Monee, IL
07 July 2026

56546643R10039